Christmas Songs for Beginning Guitar

BY PETER PENHALLOW

string letter media

PUBLISHER   David A. Lusterman

EDITOR   Jeffrey Pepper Rodgers

MANAGING EDITOR   Stacey Lynn

MUSIC EDITOR   Andrew DuBrock

DESIGNER   Barbara Summer

PRODUCTION   Judy Zimola

PRODUCTION DIRECTOR   Ellen Richman

MARKETING   Jen Fujimoto

MUSIC ENGRAVING   Peter Penhallow

COVER PHOTOGRAPH   Rory Earnshaw

AUTHOR PHOTOGRAPH   Ross Pelton

Printed in the United States of America
All rights reserved. This book was produced by String Letter Publishing, Inc.
501 Canal Blvd, Suite J, Richmond, CA 94804-3505; (510) 215-0010; www.stringletter.com

CONTENTS

The complete set of audio tracks for the musical examples and songs in *Christmas Songs for Beginning Guitar* is available for free download at **store.AcousticGuitar.com/CSBGAudio**. Just add the tracks to your shopping cart and check out to activate your free download.

INTRODUCTION

In this songbook are 15 of your favorite Christmas carols, arranged for beginning guitar. You'll learn easy versions of both the melody and the rhythm parts, so you can play these songs as guitar instrumentals or accompany singing (the complete lyrics are included for each song). The chords, keys, and techniques used are all taught in Book One of *The Acoustic Guitar Method.*

The tunes "Joy to the World," "Silent Night," and "Away in a Manger" and are among the easiest, using only three chords each. "Hark! The Herald Angels Sing," "Angels We Have Heard on High," and "We Wish You a Merry Christmas" have slightly more complex but very instructive cyclic chord progressions. "We Three Kings of Orient Are," "God Rest Ye Merry, Gentlemen," and "What Child Is This?" all are in minor keys, which we will discuss along the way. The kinds of chords,

chord progressions, rhythms, and melodies used in these songs are fundamental to countless styles of guitar music.

The audio tracks are recorded with the rhythm guitar on the left and the guitar melody on the right. You can pan your stereo left or right if you want to isolate the lead or the rhythm. For each tune, an audio track with a separate demonstration of the accompaniment pattern is included, so you can practice along before you try the whole song. Then I count you into the tune, play through it, and provide an ending. I've recorded each song twice, first up to tempo, then slowly. Playing at the slower tempo is a great way to program the moves, enabling you to gradually come up to speed. With a little practice, you should soon be entertaining your friends and family with your favorite Christmas carols.

Happy playing!

Introduction
and Tune-Up

TRACK
1

MUSIC NOTATION KEY

The music in this book is written in standard notation and tablature. Here's how to read it.

STANDARD NOTATION

Standard notation is written on a five-line staff. Notes are written in alphabetical order from A to G.

The duration of a note is determined by three things: the note head, stem, and flag. A whole note (○) equals four beats. A half note (♩) is half of that: two beats. A quarter note (♩) equals one beat, an eighth note (♪) equals half of one beat, and a 16th note (♬) is a quarter beat (there are four 16th notes per beat).

The fraction (4/4, 3/4, 6/8, etc.) or c character shown at the beginning of a piece of music denotes the time signature. The top number tells you how many beats are in each measure, and the bottom number indicates the rhythmic value of each beat (4 equals a quarter note, 8 equals an eighth note, 16 equals a 16th note, and 2 equals a half note). The most common time signature is 4/4, which signifies four quarter notes per measure and is sometimes designated with the symbol c (for common time). The symbol ¢ stands for cut time (2/2). Most songs are either in 4/4 or 3/4.

TABLATURE

In tablature, the six horizontal lines represent the six strings of the guitar, with the first string on the top and sixth on the bottom. The numbers refer to fret numbers on a given string. The notation and tablature in this book are designed to be used in tandem—refer to the notation to get the rhythmic information and note durations, and refer to the tablature to get the exact locations of the notes on the guitar fingerboard.

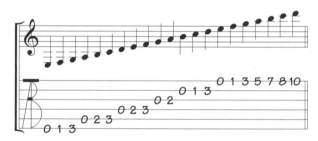

FINGERINGS

Fingerings are indicated with small numbers and letters in the notation. Fretting-hand fingering is indicated with 1 for the index finger, 2 the middle, 3 the ring, 4 the pinky, and *T* the thumb. Picking-hand fingering is indicated by *i* for the index finger, *m* the middle, *a* the ring, *c* the pinky, and *p* the thumb. Circled numbers indicate the string the note is played on. Remember that the fingerings indicated are only suggestions; if you find a different way that works better for you, use it.

CHORD DIAGRAMS

Chord diagrams show where the fingers go on the fingerboard. Frets are shown horizontally. The thick top line represents the nut. A Roman numeral to the right of a diagram indicates a chord played higher up the neck (in this case the top horizontal line is thin). Strings are shown as vertical lines. The line on the far left represents the sixth (lowest) string, and the line on the far right represents the first (highest) string. Dots show where the fingers go, and thick horizontal lines indicate barres. Numbers above the diagram are left-hand finger numbers, as used in standard notation. Again, the fingerings are only suggestions. An *X* indicates a string that should be muted or not played; 0 indicates an open string.

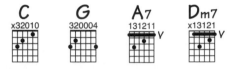

CAPOS

If a capo is used, a Roman numeral indicates the fret where the capo should be placed. The standard notation and tablature is written as if the capo were the nut of the guitar. For instance, a tune capoed anywhere up the neck and played using key-of-G chord shapes and fingerings will be written in the key of G. Likewise, open strings held down by the capo are written as open strings.

TUNINGS

Alternate guitar tunings are given from the lowest (sixth) string to the highest (first) string. For instance, D A D G B E indicates standard tuning with the bottom string dropped to D. Standard notation for songs in alternate tunings always reflects the actual pitches of the notes. Arrows underneath tuning notes indicate strings that are altered from standard tuning and whether they are tuned up or down.

VOCAL TUNES

Vocal tunes are sometimes written with a fully tabbed-out introduction and a vocal melody with chord diagrams for the rest of the piece. The tab intro is usually your indication of which strum or fingerpicking pattern to use in the rest of the piece. The melody with lyrics underneath is the melody sung by the vocalist. Occasionally, smaller notes are written with the melody to indicate the harmony part sung by another vocalist. These are not to be confused with cue notes, which are small notes that indicate melodies that vary when a section is repeated. Listen to a recording of the piece to get a feel for the guitar accompaniment and to hear the singing if you aren't skilled at reading vocal melodies.

ARTICULATIONS

There are a number of ways you can articulate a note on the guitar. Notes connected with slurs (not to be confused with ties) in the tablature or standard notation are articulated with either a hammer-on, pull-off, or slide. Lower notes slurred to higher notes are played as hammer-ons; higher notes slurred to lower notes are played as pull-offs. While it's usually obvious that slurred notes are played as hammer-ons or pull-offs, an *H* or *P* is included above the tablature as an extra reminder.

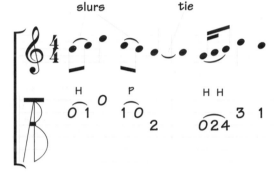

Slides are represented with a dash, and an *S* is included above the tab. A dash preceding a note represents a slide into the note from an indefinite point in the direction of the slide; a dash following a note indicates a slide off of the note to an indefinite point in the direction of the slide. For two slurred notes connected with a slide, you should pick the first note and then slide into the second.

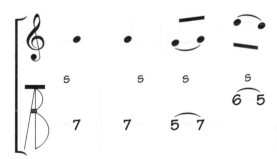

Bends are represented with upward curves, as shown in the next example. Most bends have a specific destination pitch—the number above the bend symbol shows how much the bend raises the string's pitch: 1/4 for a slight bend, 1/2 for a half step, 1 for a whole step.

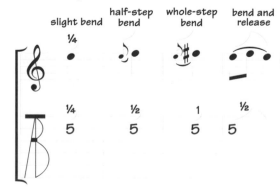

Grace notes are represented by small notes with a dash through the stem in standard notation and with small numbers in the tab. A grace note is a very quick ornament leading into a note, most commonly executed as a hammer-on, pull-off, or slide. In the following example, pluck the note at the fifth fret on the beat, then quickly hammer onto the seventh fret. The second example is executed as a quick pull-off from the second fret to the open string. In the third example, both notes at the fifth fret are played simultaneously (even though it appears that the fifth fret, fourth string, is to be played by itself), then the seventh fret, fourth string, is quickly hammered.

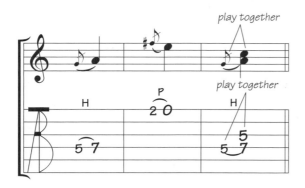

HARMONICS

Harmonics are represented by diamond-shaped notes in the standard notation and a small dot next to the tablature numbers. Natural harmonics are indicated with the text "Harmonics" or "Harm." above the tablature. Harmonics articulated with the right hand (often called artificial harmonics) include the text "R.H. Harmonics" or "R.H. Harm." above the tab. Right-hand harmonics are executed by lightly touching the harmonic node (usually 12 frets above the open string or fretted note) with the right-hand index finger and plucking the string with the thumb or ring finger or pick. For extended phrases played with right-hand harmonics, the fretted notes are shown in the tab along with instructions to touch the harmonics 12 frets above the notes.

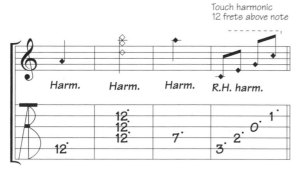

REPEATS

One of the most confusing parts of a musical score can be the navigation symbols, such as repeats, *D.S. al Coda, D.C. al Fine, To Coda,* etc.

Repeat symbols are placed at the beginning and end of the passage to be repeated.

You should ignore repeat symbols with the dots on the right side the first time you encounter them; when you come to a repeat symbol with dots on the left side, jump back to the previous repeat symbol facing the opposite direction (if there is no previous symbol, go to the beginning of the piece). The next time you come to the repeat symbol, ignore it and keep going unless it includes instructions such as "Repeat three times."

Often a section will have a different ending after each repeat. The example below includes a first and a second ending. Play until you hit the repeat symbol, jump back to the previous repeat symbol and play until you reach the bracketed first ending, skip the measures under the bracket and jump immediately to the second ending, and then continue.

D.S. stands for *dal segno* or "from the sign." When you encounter this indication, jump immediately to the sign (𝄋).

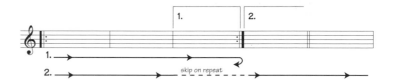

D.S. is usually accompanied by *al Fine* or *al Coda. Fine* indicates the end of a piece. A coda is a final passage near the end of a piece and is indicated with (⊕). *D.S. al Coda* simply tells you to jump back to the sign and continue on until you are instructed to jump to the coda, indicated with *To Coda* (⊕). ⊕

D.C. stands for *da capo* or "from the beginning." Jump to the top of the piece when you encounter this indication.

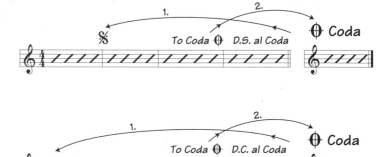

D.C. al Fine tells you to jump to the beginning of a tune and continue until you encounter the *Fine* indicating the end of the piece (ignore the *Fine* the first time through).

JINGLE BELLS

Written in 1857 by James Pierpont, "Jingle Bells" was originally a Thanksgiving children's production. (It was first referred to as "a merry little jingle" by one of Pierpont's neighbors, who had the only piano in town.) The community is said to have liked it so much that they asked the children to repeat it at Christmas. It has been a holiday favorite ever since.

The accompaniment pattern shown below is used throughout this book: a bass note followed by a strum. In a song like this with a 4/4 time signature (that's four beats per measure, also known as *common time*), you play that bass/strum pattern twice in each measure. You can play with a pick or, if you prefer to use your right-hand fingers, alternate between your thumb for the bass notes and the other fingers for the strum. Note that the G-chord fingering shown uses your ring finger on the sixth string, middle finger on the fifth string,

and pinky on the first string, which makes it a little easier to switch to the other chords. If you prefer, you can play the G with your middle finger on the sixth string, index on the fifth string, and ring finger on the first string.

You can also use either a pick or your fingers to play the melodies. If you use a pick, as I typically do, try using it in a continuous down-up pattern. For your fretting hand, most of the melodies in this book can be achieved with the first three fingers. The left-hand fingering suggestions in the notation might help you play the melodies more smoothly: 1 means your index finger, 2 the middle, 3 the ring, and 4 the pinky. Generally speaking, you should use your index finger for notes at the first fret, middle finger for notes on the second fret, and ring finger for notes on the third fret and higher. Exceptions to this are indicated in the notation. ◆

G
1. DASHING THROUGH THE SNOW IN A ONE-HORSE OPEN SLEIGH
                    D7   G
   O'ER THE FIELDS WE GO LAUGHING ALL THE WAY (HA HA HA)
                    C
   BELLS ON BOB-TAIL RING MAKING SPIRITS BRIGHT
                    G   D7   G
   WHAT FUN IT IS TO RIDE AND SING A SLEIGHING SONG TONIGHT

          D7 G
   OH JINGLE BELLS, JINGLE BELLS, JINGLE ALL THE WAY
   C   G   D7
   OH WHAT FUN IT IS TO RIDE IN A ONE-HORSE OPEN SLEIGH
          G
   HEY, JINGLE BELLS, JINGLE BELLS, JINGLE ALL THE WAY
   C   G   D7   G
   OH WHAT FUN IT IS TO RIDE IN A ONE-HORSE OPEN SLEIGH

                                G   C
2. A DAY OR TWO AGO I THOUGHT I'D TAKE A RIDE
                              D7   G
   AND SOON MISS FANNY BRIGHT WAS SEATED BY MY SIDE
                                                    C
   THE HORSE WAS LEAN AND LANK, MISFORTUNE SEEMED HIS LOT
                              G   D7   G
   HE GOT INTO A DRIFTED BANK AND WE, WE GOT UPSOT

   CHORUS

9

JOY TO THE WORLD

Around 1800, Lowell Mason, a Boston composer and music publisher, found Isaac Watts' poem of "joy" and set it to music. Watts, superintendent of Boston's schools, was a pioneer in music education.

This song uses the same key and strum pattern as "Jingle Bells." The key represents the tonal center of the song. The first and last chords are often, but not always, the same as the key of the song. This is a classic three-chord song, with just G, C, and D7. "Joy to the World" is usually performed in grand classical style, but let's play it here campfire style, with a folky rhythm. ✦

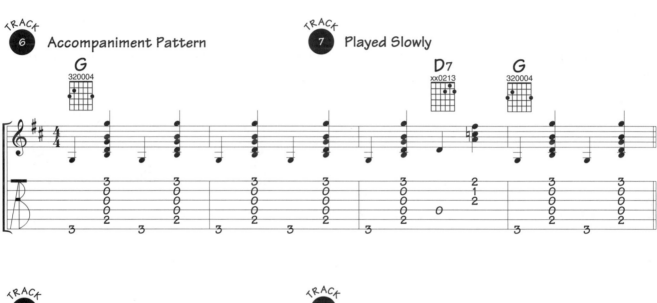

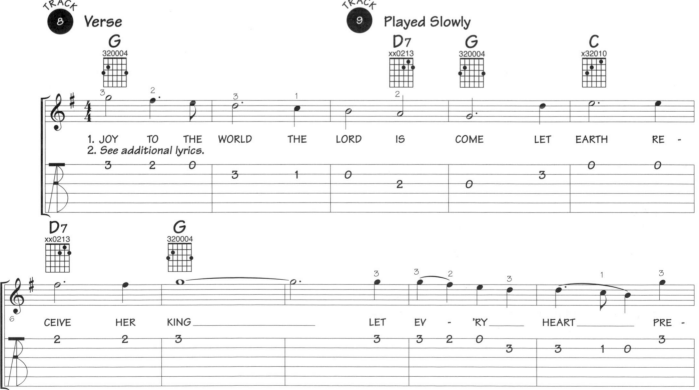

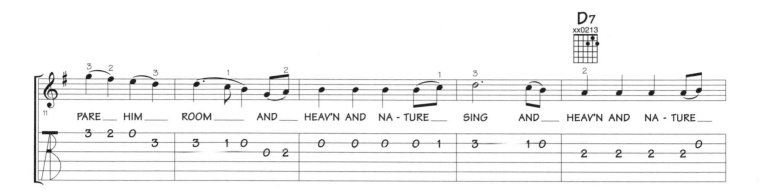

PARE___ HIM___ ROOM___ AND___ HEAV'N AND NA - TURE___ SING AND___ HEAV'N AND NA - TURE___

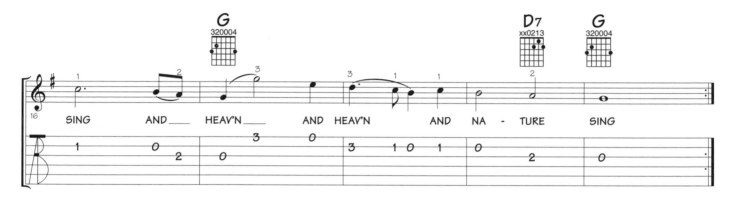

SING AND___ HEAV'N___ AND HEAV'N AND NA - TURE SING

G   D7 G
1. JOY TO THE WORLD, THE LORD IS COME
      C   D7   G
   LET EARTH RECEIVE HER KING

   LET EVERY HEART PREPARE HIM ROOM

   AND HEAV'N AND NATURE SING
      D7
   AND HEAV'N AND NATURE SING
      G   D7 G
   AND HEAV'N AND HEAV'N AND NATURE SING

G   D7 G
2. JOY TO THE EARTH, THE SAVIOR REIGNS
      C   D7   G
   LET MEN THEIR SONGS EMPLOY

   WHILE FIELDS AND FLOODS, ROCKS, HILLS, AND PLAINS

   REPEAT THE SOUNDING JOY
      D7
   REPEAT THE SOUNDING JOY
      G   D7 G
   REPEAT, REPEAT THE SOUNDING JOY

DECK THE HALLS

Ideas for many classical songs came from folk melodies. Mozart used this decidedly festive old Welsh melody in a duet for piano and violin. Legend has it that the "fa-la-la" parts came from medieval minstrels who used such phrases when they did not know the words, but as it turns out, the words are actually of 19th-century American origin.

Once again we're using a bass note/strum pattern, in the key of G. Notice that in this song the first two lines are identical, the third deviates, and the fourth is like the first two, with a

different ending. Picking up on these kinds of repetitions makes a song easier to learn. The Am7 chord might be new to you, but it's nice and simple: just hold an Am chord and then lift your ring finger off the third string to play it open.

There are a couple of fast phrases in the melody, particularly the "fa-la-la" part. Practice picking with the down-up motion, sometimes referred to as *double picking* or *alternate picking,* and these parts should soon become easy.   ✦

12

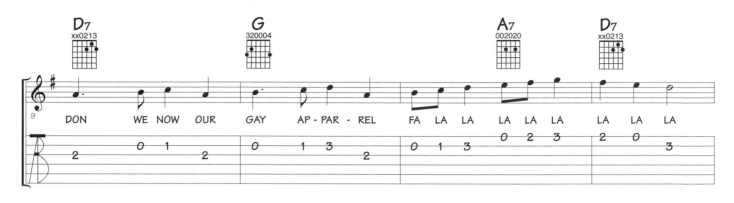

DON WE NOW OUR GAY AP - PAR - REL FA LA LA LA LA LA LA LA LA

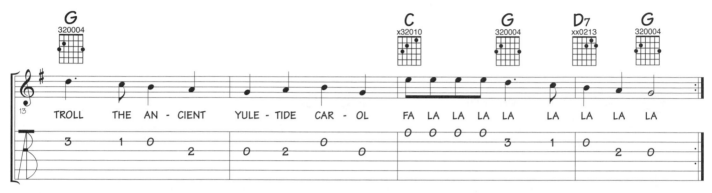

TROLL THE AN - CIENT YULE - TIDE CAR - OL FA LA LA LA LA LA LA LA LA

G
1. DECK THE HALLS WITH BOUGHS OF HOLLY
   Am7   G   D7 G
   FA LA LA LA LA, LA LA LA LA

   'TIS THE SEASON TO BE JOLLY
   Am7   G   D7 G
   FA LA LA LA LA, LA LA LA LA
   D7   G
   DON WE NOW OUR GAY APPAREL
         A7   D7
   FA LA LA, LA LA LA, LA LA LA
   G
   TROLL THE ANCIENT YULETIDE CAROL
   C   G   D7 G
   FA LA LA LA LA, LA LA LA LA

   G
2. SEE THE BLAZING YULE BEFORE US
   Am7   G   D7 G
   FA LA LA LA LA, LA LA LA LA

   STRIKE THE HARP AND JOIN THE CHORUS
   Am7   G   D7 G
   FA LA LA LA LA, LA LA LA LA
   D7   G
   FOLLOW ME IN MERRY MEASURE
          A7   D7
   FA LA LA, LA LA LA, LA LA LA
   G
   WHILE I TELL OF YULETIDE TREASURES
   C   G   D7 G
   FA LA LA LA LA, LA LA LA LA

   G
3. FAST AWAY THE OLD YEAR PASSES
   Am7   G   D7 G
   FA LA LA LA LA, LA LA LA LA

   HAIL THE NEW, YE LADS AND LASSES
   Am7   G   D7 G
   FA LA LA LA LA, LA LA LA LA
   D7   G
   SING WE JOYOUS ALL TOGETHER
          A7   D7
   FA LA LA, LA LA LA, LA LA LA
   G
   HEEDLESS OF THE WIND AND WEATHER
   C   G   D7 G
   FA LA LA LA LA, LA LA LA LA

SILENT NIGHT

Joseph Mohr, an assistant pastor, wrote a poem called "Stille Nacht" that was meant for Christmas Eve service. The organ, however, was broken. Franz Gruber, the church organist, composed the melody and arranged it for voice and guitar on the spot, just in time for midnight mass. So this beautiful song came into being back in 1818.

So far, we've been playing in 4/4 time, or common time. This tune introduces a new time signature: 3/4, or three beats per measure, most commonly found in a waltz. The strum pattern therefore is different: one bass note followed by two strums. We introduce a new key, E, which is very much a guitar key, and the B7 chord.

In the melody on measure 18, try using your pinky on the fifth fret of the high E string. This song should be played quietly, like a lullaby. In music terminology, derived from the Italian, quietly is referred to as *piano*. ✦

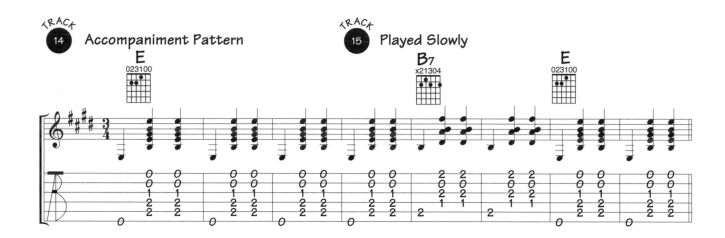

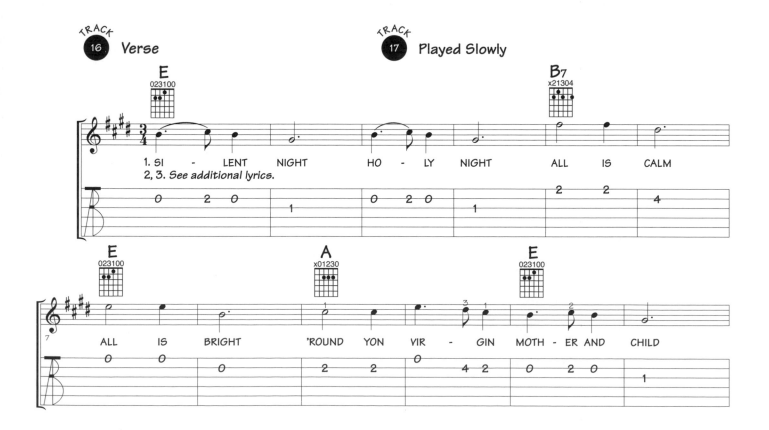

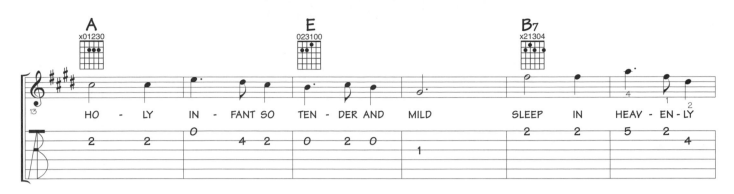

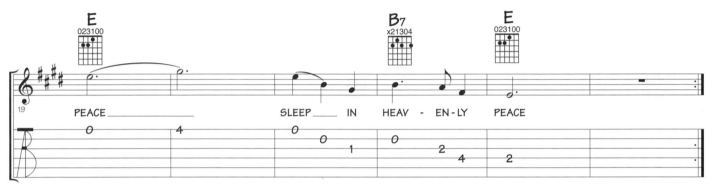

E
1. SILENT NIGHT, HOLY NIGHT
   B7   E
   ALL IS CALM, ALL IS BRIGHT
   A   E
   'ROUND YON VIRGIN MOTHER AND CHILD
   A   E
   HOLY INFANT SO TENDER AND MILD
   B7   E
   SLEEP IN HEAVENLY PEACE
            B7   E
   SLEEP IN HEAVENLY PEACE

   E
2. SILENT NIGHT, HOLY NIGHT
   B7   E
   SHEPHERDS QUAKE AT THE SIGHT
   A   E
   GLORIES STREAM FROM HEAVENS AFAR
   A   E
   HEAVENLY HOSTS SING ALLELUIA
   B7   E
   CHRIST THE SAVIOR IS BORN
            B7   E
   CHRIST THE SAVIOR IS BORN

   E
3. SILENT NIGHT, HOLY NIGHT
   B7   E
   SON OF GOD, LOVE'S PURE LIGHT
   A   E
   RADIANT BEAMS FROM THY HOLY FACE
   A   E
   WITH THE DAWN OF REDEEMING GRACE
   B7   E
   JESUS, LORD, AT THY BIRTH
            B7   E
   JESUS, LORD, AT THY BIRTH

THE FIRST NOEL

The words and music to "The First Noel" are traditional. Some say the origins are French, others English. The song was collected in William Sandy's *Christmas Carols Ancient and Modern* in 1833.

Like "Silent Night," "The First Noel" is in 3/4, this time in the key of D, and uses a similar bass/strum/strum pattern. In all the previous songs, the melodies start on beat 1 of measure 1. This song begins with a *pickup* (in traditional music referred to as an *anacrusis*) before the first beat, on beat 3 of the previous measure. For this entire song, fret the notes at the second fret with your index finger, at the third fret with your middle finger, and at the fourth fret with your ring finger. ✦

TRACK 18 Accompaniment Pattern

TRACK 19 Played Slowly

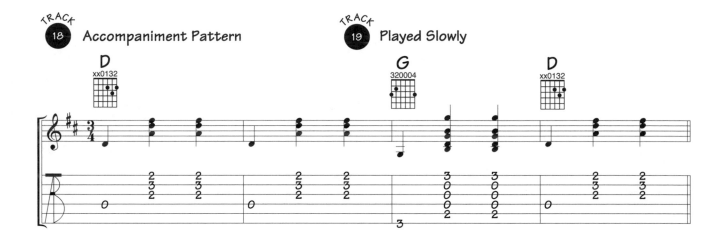

TRACK 20 Verse

TRACK 21 Played Slowly

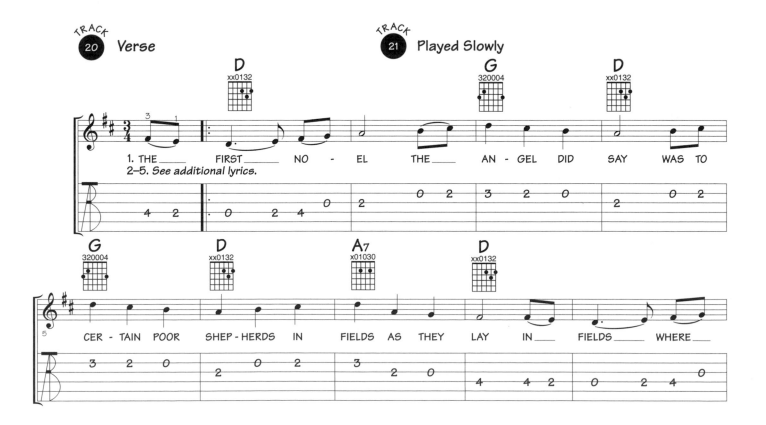

1. THE FIRST NO - EL THE AN - GEL DID SAY WAS TO
2–5. *See additional lyrics.*

CER - TAIN POOR SHEP - HERDS IN FIELDS AS THEY LAY IN FIELDS WHERE

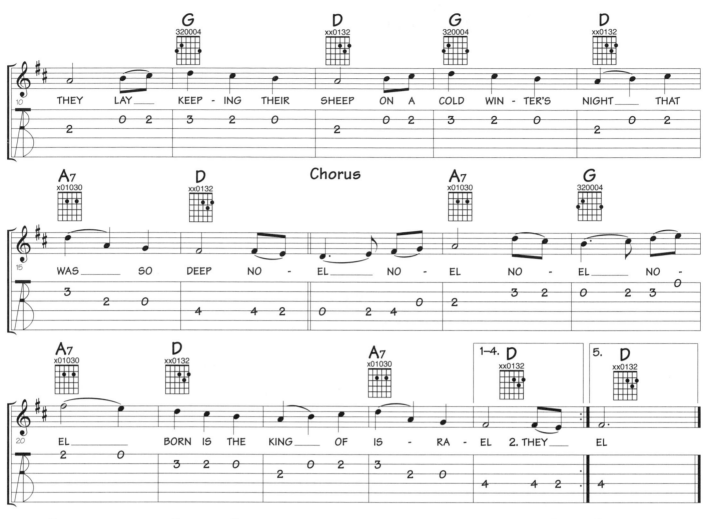

1.   D   G   D
    THE FIRST NOEL, THE ANGEL DID SAY
             G   D   A7   D
    WAS TO CERTAIN POOR SHEPHERDS IN FIELDS WHERE THEY LAY
                         G   D
    IN FIELDS WHERE THEY LAY KEEPING THEIR SHEEP
               G   D   A7   D
    ON A COLD WINTER'S NIGHT THAT WAS SO DEEP

                      A7   G   A7
    NOEL, NOEL, NOEL, NOEL
    D   A7   D
    BORN IS THE KING OF ISRAEL

                      G   D
2. THEY LOOKED UP AND SAW A STAR
             G   D   A7   D
    SHINING IN THE EAST BEYOND THEM FAR
                 G   D
    AND TO THE EARTH IT GAVE GREAT LIGHT
               G   D   A7   D
    AND SO IT CONTINUED BOTH DAY AND NIGHT

             CHORUS

                       G   D
3. AND BY THE LIGHT OF THAT SAME STAR
             G   D   A7   D
    THREE WISE MEN CAME FROM A COUNTRY FAR

                                               G   D
    TO SEEK FOR A KING WAS THEIR INTENT
                   G   D   A7   D
    AND TO FOLLOW THE STAR WHEREVER IT WENT

        CHORUS

                                G   D
4. THIS STAR DREW NIGH TO THE NORTHWEST
            G   D   A7   D
    O'ER BETHLEHEM IT TOOK ITS REST
                         G   D
    AND THERE IT DID BOTH STOP AND STAY
            G   D   A7   D
    RIGHT OVER THE PLACE WHERE JESUS LAY

        CHORUS

                              G   D
5. THEN ENTERED IN THOSE WISE MEN THREE
            G   D   A7   D
    FULL REVERENTLY UPON THEIR KNEE
                         G   D
    AND OFFERED THERE IN HIS PRESENCE
            G   D   A7   D
    THEIR GOLD AND MYRRH AND FRANKINCENSE

        CHORUS

AWAY IN A MANGER

The words to "Away in a Manger" are generally considered to be American, author unknown, though some attribute them to James R. Murray, who published the song in a children's songbook in the 1880s. Two different melodies are commonly associated with this piece. One is an old German folk song that some credit to Murray, and the other is the Scottish song "Flow Gently, Sweet Afton." I learned the tune from children I have worked with in Christmas productions, and it is a nice, easy folk arrangement.

The time signature is 3/4, and we are in the key of A. In the melody part, notice that in measures 8–9 you can simply hold down an A fingering to play those successive notes on the second fret of the fourth, third, and second strings. ◆

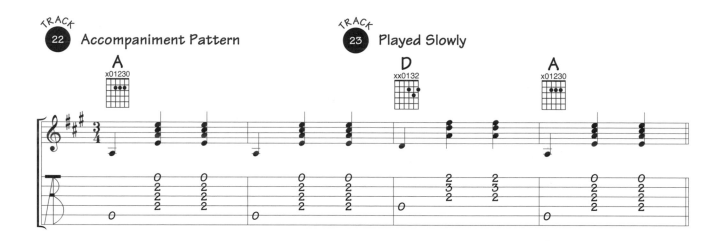

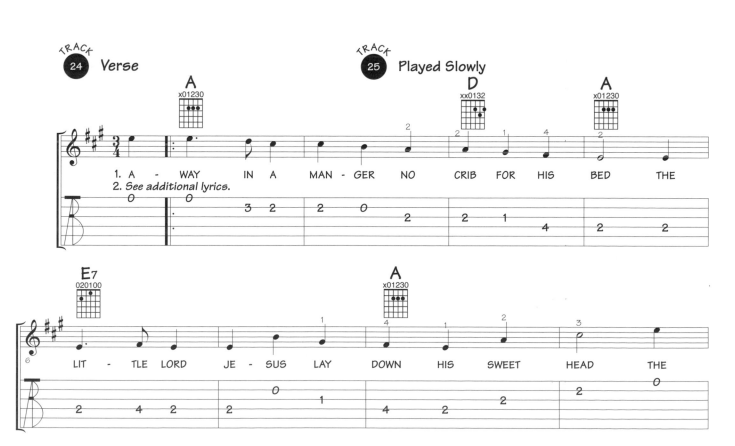

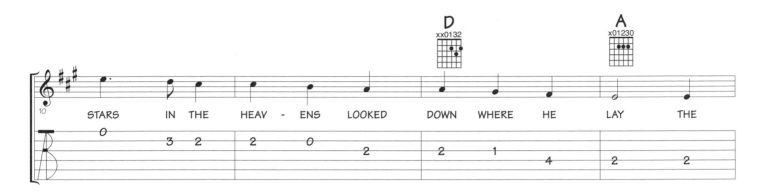

STARS IN THE HEAV - ENS LOOKED DOWN WHERE HE LAY THE

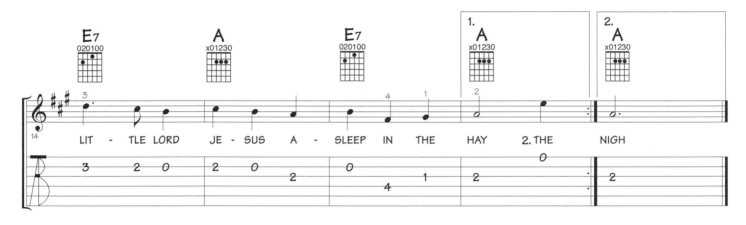

LIT - TLE LORD JE - SUS A - SLEEP IN THE HAY 2. THE NIGH

```
           A                    D        A
1. AWAY IN A MANGER, NO CRIB FOR HIS BED
       E7                    A
   THE LITTLE LORD JESUS LAY DOWN HIS SWEET HEAD
                               D        A
   THE STARS IN THE HEAVENS LOOKED DOWN WHERE HE LAY
       E7        A    E7       A
   THE LITTLE LORD JESUS ASLEEP IN THE HAY
```

```
           A                    D        A
2. THE CATTLE ARE LOWING, THE POOR BABY WAKES
       E7                    A
   BUT LITTLE LORD JESUS NO CRYING HE MAKES
                                D        A
   I LOVE THEE LORD JESUS, LOOK DOWN FROM THE SKY
       E7        A    E7       A
   AND STAY BY MY CRADLE TILL MORNING IS NIGH
```

O CHRISTMAS TREE

The traditional German Christmas carol "O Tannenbaum" is sung in English as "O Christmas Tree." Its origins are uncertain, but since the Middle Ages it has been sung in Germany and Austria, where the popular custom of decorating evergreen trees began. The melody has proved so popular that four states use it for their state song.

The time signature is 3/4. Notice that in the third measure of the accompaniment pattern, you play one short strum (one beat) and one sustained strum (two beats). This pattern is used in measures 3, 7, and 18. Measure 14 includes an E7 chord, which you play by making a regular E chord and lifting your third finger off the fourth string. ✦

20

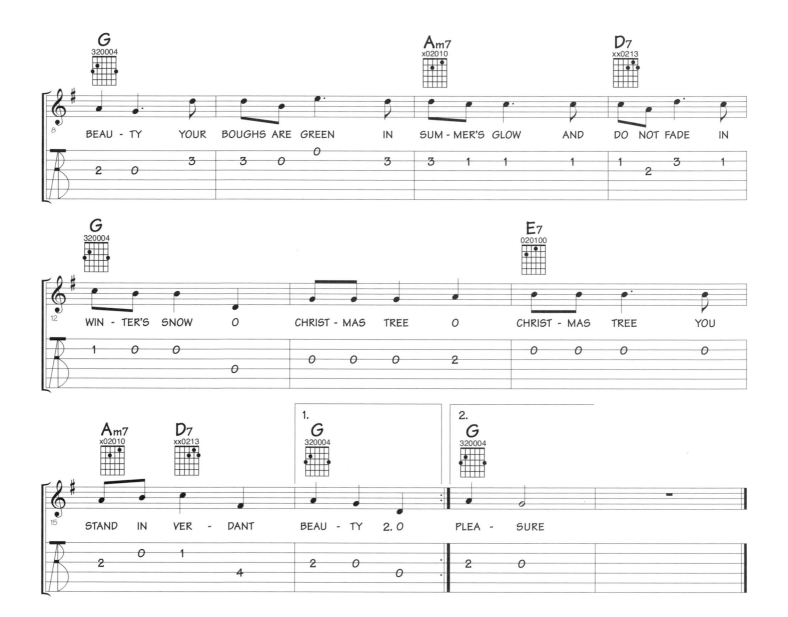

G   Em
1. O CHRISTMAS TREE, O CHRISTMAS TREE
  Am7 D7   G
YOU STAND IN VERDANT BEAUTY
         Em
O CHRISTMAS TREE, O CHRISTMAS TREE
  Am7 D7   G
YOU STAND IN VERDANT BEAUTY
            Am7
YOUR BOUGHS ARE GREEN IN SUMMER'S GLOW
  D7   G
AND DO NOT FADE IN WINTER'S SNOW
          E7
O CHRISTMAS TREE, O CHRISTMAS TREE
  Am7 D7   G
YOU STAND IN VERDANT BEAUTY

G   Em
2. O CHRISTMAS TREE, O CHRISTMAS TREE
  Am7 D7   G
YOU GIVE US SO MUCH PLEASURE
         Em
O CHRISTMAS TREE, O CHRISTMAS TREE
  Am7 D7   G
YOU GIVE US SO MUCH PLEASURE
            Am7
HOW OFT AT CHRISTMASTIDE THE SIGHT
  D7   G
O GREEN FIR TREE GIVES US DELIGHT
          E7
O CHRISTMAS TREE, O CHRISTMAS TREE
  Am7 D7   G
YOU GIVE US SO MUCH PLEASURE

O COME ALL YE FAITHFUL

This song boasts many sources. It is most likely a Latin hymn, "Adeste Fideles," with words written by John Francis Wade in the 1740s. The Latin version has irregular lines and no rhyme.

"O Come All Ye Faithful" brings us back to 4/4 once again.

The main accompaniment pattern is bass note/strum. The second example indicates how to treat the *cadence,* or ending, that sums up the tune.

The chords move a little more quickly in this song, and you will find several seventh chords in here (D7, A7, Am7) that add a little more spice. Just take the changes slowly at first to get them under your fingers. ✦

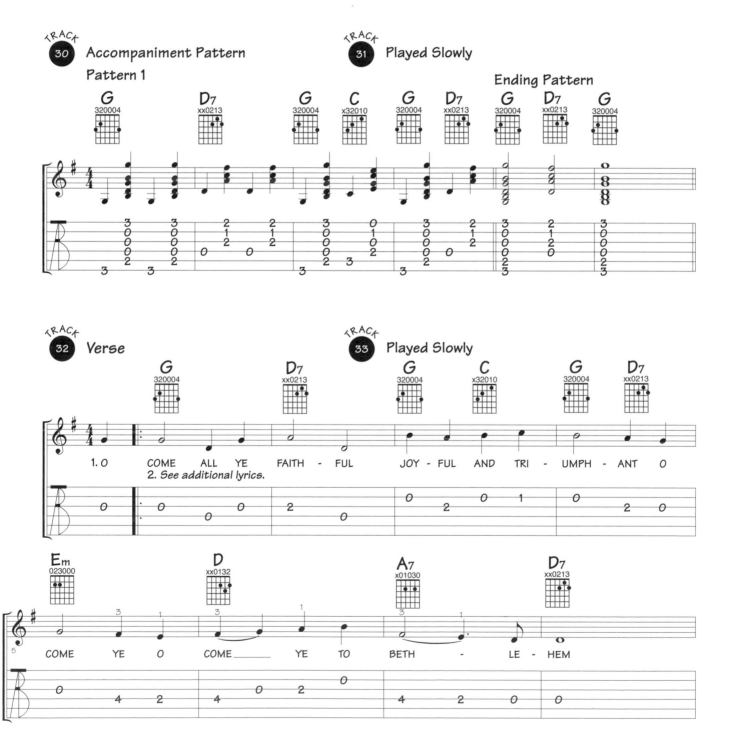

22

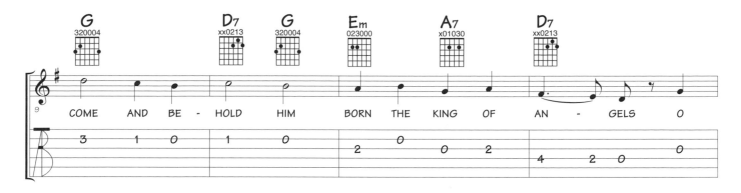

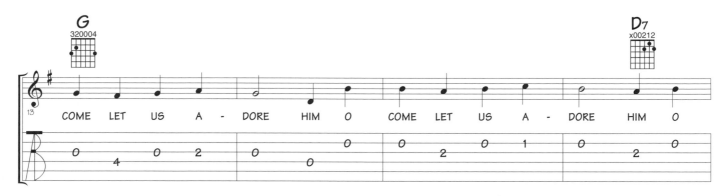

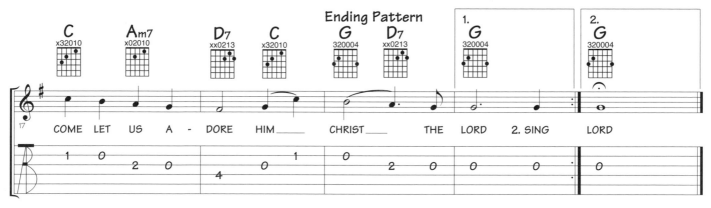

	G		D7		G	C		G	D7

1. O COME ALL YE FAITHFUL, JOYFUL AND TRIUMPHANT
   Em   D   A7   D7
   O COME YE, O COME YE, TO BETHLEHEM
   G   D7 G Em   A7   D7
   COME AND BEHOLD HIM, BORN THE KING OF ANGELS
     G
   O COME LET US ADORE HIM
               D7
   O COME LET US ADORE HIM
     C   Am7 D7   C
   O COME LET US ADORE HIM
   G D7   G
   CHRIST THE LORD

2. SING CHOIRS OF ANGELS, SING IN EXULTATION
   Em   D   A7   D7
   O SING, ALL YE CITIZENS OF HEAVEN ABOVE
   G   D7 G Em A7   D7
   GLORY TO GOD IN THE HIGHEST
     G
   O COME LET US ADORE HIM
               D7
   O COME LET US ADORE HIM
     C   Am7 D7   C
   O COME LET US ADORE HIM
   G D7   G
   CHRIST THE LORD

HARK! THE HERALD ANGELS SING

In 1739, Charles Wesley (brother of John Wesley, founder of the Methodist church), wrote the words to this song. Wesley's friend George Whitefield rewrote the opening line, replacing the original "Hark, how the heaven rings." In 1840, Mendelssohn wrote a cantata intended for secular use, specifically in commemoration of Johannes Gutenberg and the invention of printing. Although Wesley was adamant that the music to his song be slow and solemn, William Cummings married

Mendelssohn's music with Wesley's words in 1855 to create this upbeat Christmas favorite.

The song begins with a basic three-chord progression in the key of G and then gets a little busier. Once again, we're using a good number of seventh chords, especially D7, which leads nicely back to G. ✦

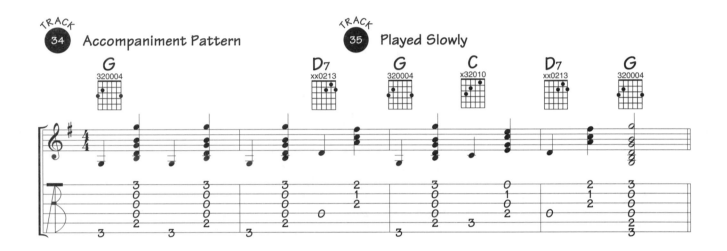

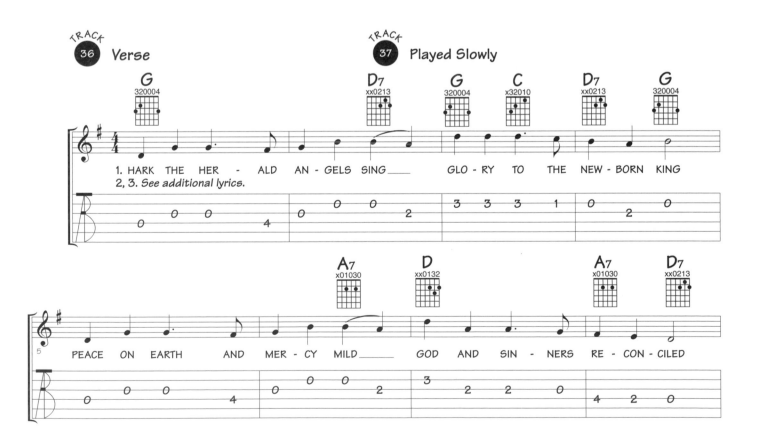

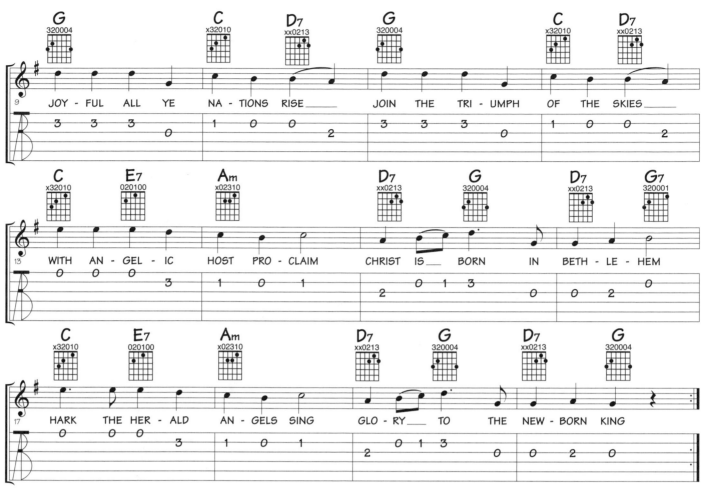

1.
```
G                           D7
HARK! THE HERALD ANGELS SING
G      C    D7       G
GLORY TO THE NEWBORN KING
                          A7
PEACE ON EARTH AND MERCY MILD
D            A7    D7
GOD AND SINNERS RECONCILED
G              C      D7
JOYFUL ALL YE NATIONS RISE
G                 C      D7
JOIN THE TRIUMPH OF THE SKIES
C      E7    Am
WITH ANGELIC HOST PROCLAIM
D7     G     D7    G7
CHRIST IS BORN IN BETHLEHEM
C      E7    Am
HARK! THE HERALD ANGELS SING
D7   G    D7      G
GLORY TO THE NEWBORN KING
```

2.
```
G                           D7
CHRIST, BY HIGHEST HEAV'N ADORED
G      C  D7      G
CHRIST, THE EVERLASTING LORD
                        A7
LATE IN TIME BEHOLD HIM COME
D            A7    D7
OFFSPRING OF A VIRGIN WOMB
G                 C    D7
VEIL'D IN FLESH, THE GODHEAD SEE
```

```
G                    C   D7
HAIL, TH'INCARNATE DEITY
C           E7         Am
PLEASED, AS MAN, WITH MEN TO DWELL,
D7     G      D7  G7
JESUS, OUR EMMANUEL!
C           E7         Am
HARK! THE HERALD ANGELS SING
D7   G    D7      G
GLORY TO THE NEWBORN KING
```

3.
```
G                                D7
HAIL! THE HEAV'N-BORN PRINCE OF PEACE
G      C    D7       G
HAIL! THE SON OF RIGHTEOUSNESS
                          A7
LIGHT AND LIFE TO ALL HE BRINGS
D            A7    D7
RISEN WITH HEALING IN HIS WINGS
G              C      D7
MILD HE LAYS HIS GLORY BY
G              C      D7
BORN THAT MAN NO MORE MAY DIE
C      E7    Am
BORN TO RAISE THE SONS OF EARTH,
D7     G     D7    G7
BORN TO GIVE THEM SECOND BIRTH
C      E7    Am
HARK! THE HERALD ANGELS SING
D7   G    D7      G
GLORY TO THE NEWBORN KING
```

IT CAME UPON A MIDNIGHT CLEAR

This is a true American Christmas carol. The words are from a poem written in 1849 by Unitarian minister Dr. Edmund Sears. The words were later added to the melody "Carol," written by Richard Storrs Willis, an editor at the *New York Tribune*.

We come back to the waltz or 3/4 rhythm: one bass note followed by two strums. The inclusion of the B7 and Em in measures 17–19 makes for a dramatic turning point leading

into the final line. In the melody part, using your pinky for the notes on the fourth fret in those same measures will make things smoother. This song should not plod but whisk by, in true waltz style. ◆

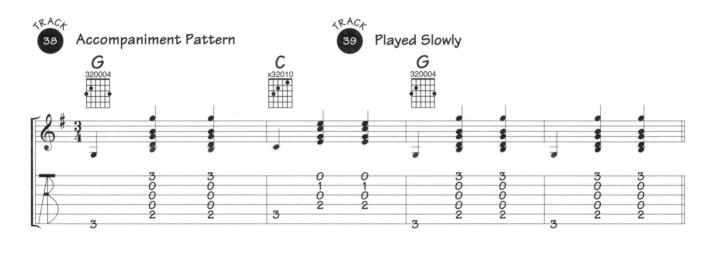

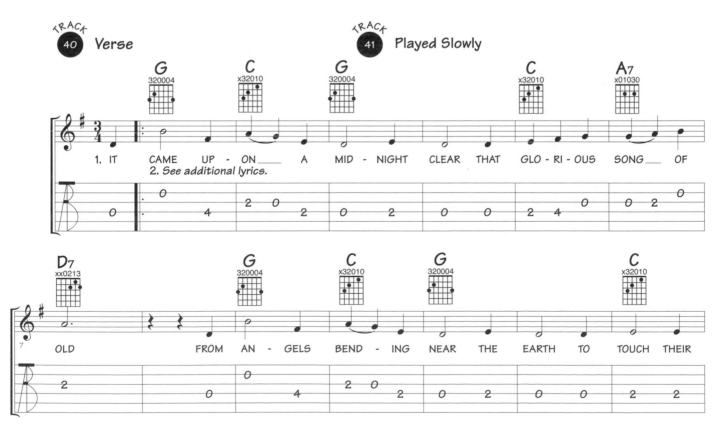

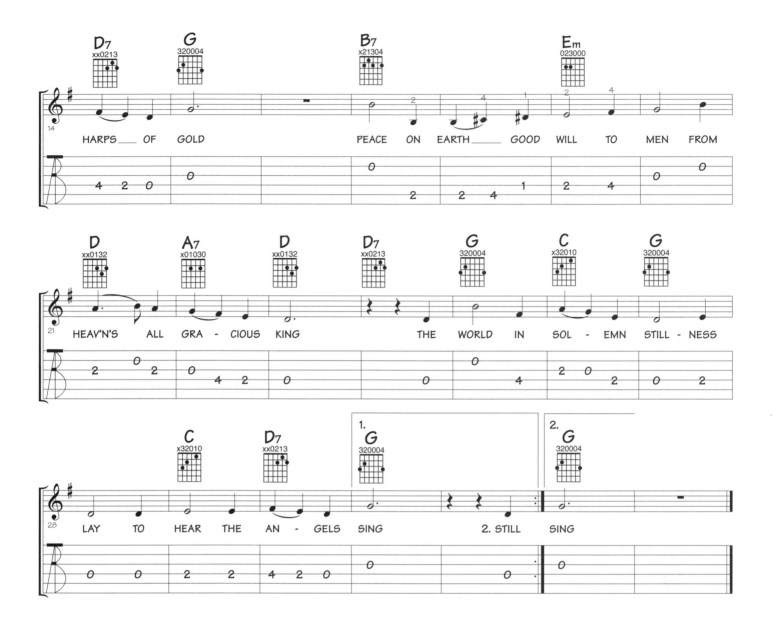

1. IT CAME UPON A MIDNIGHT CLEAR
    G   C   G

    C   A7   D
THAT GLORIOUS SONG OF OLD
    G   C   G
FROM ANGELS BENDING NEAR THE EARTH
    C   D7   G
TO TOUCH THEIR HARPS OF GOLD
B7   Em
PEACE ON EARTH, GOOD WILL TO MEN
    D   A7   D D7
FROM HEAV'N'S ALL-GRACIOUS KING
    G   C   G
THE WORLD IN SOLEMN STILLNESS LAY
    C   D7   G
TO HEAR THE ANGELS SING

2. STILL THROUGH THE CLOVEN SKIES THEY CAME
    G   C   G

    C   A7   D
WITH PEACEFUL WINGS UNFURLED
    G   C   G
AND STILL THEIR HEAVENLY MUSIC FLOATS
    C   D7   G
O'ER ALL THE WEARY WORLD
B7   Em
ABOVE ITS SAD AND LOWLY PLAINS
    D   A7   D D7
THEY BEND ON HOVERING WING
    G   C   G
AND EVER O'ER ITS BABEL SOUNDS
    C   D7   G
THE BLESSED ANGELS SING

WHAT CHILD IS THIS?

This melody is, of course, "Greensleeves," a beautiful pre-Elizabethan folk song. It is said that Henry VIII wrote lyrics to "Greensleeves," but the words to "What Child Is This?" were extrapolated from William Chatterton Dix's "The Manger Throne" (1865).

Once again, we have the time signature of 3/4. Notice the new accompaniment pattern: it is simply one strum per measure. We also introduce a minor key (E minor). The darker sound of the minor is offset in this song by the move to G major in measure 17. ✦

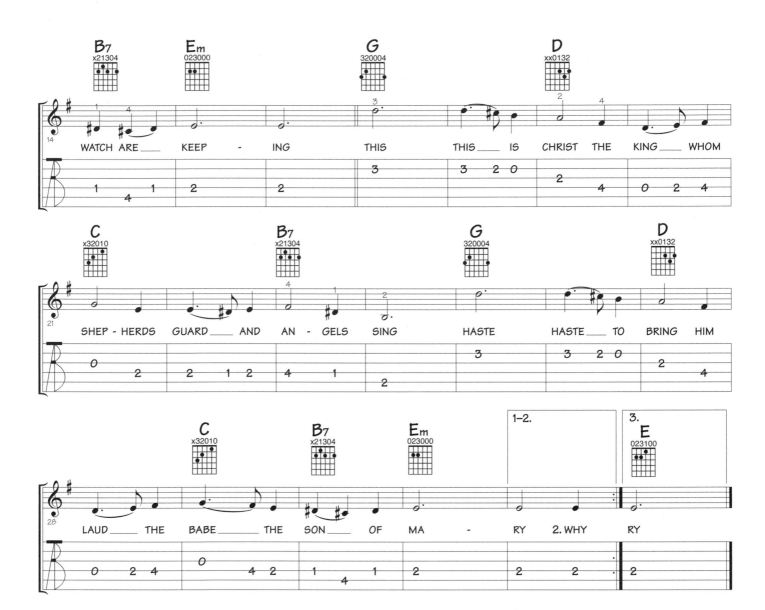

Em   D
1. WHAT CHILD IS THIS WHO LAID TO REST
    C   B7
ON MARY'S LAP IS SLEEPING?
      Em   D
WHOM ANGELS GREET WITH ANTHEMS SWEET
     C   B7   Em
WHILE SHEPHERDS WATCH ARE KEEPING
  G   D
THIS, THIS IS CHRIST, THE KING
      C   B7
WHOM SHEPHERDS GUARD AND ANGELS SING
  G   D
HASTE, HASTE TO BRING HIM LAUD
    C   B7   Em
THE BABE, THE SON OF MARY

  Em   D
2. WHY LIES HE IN SUCH MEAN ESTATE
      C   B7
WHERE OX AND ASS ARE FEEDING?
     Em   D
WHOM CHRISTIAN FEAR, FOR SINNERS HERE
    C   B7   Em
THE SILENT WORD IS PLEADING

  G   D
NAILS, SPEARS SHALL PIERCE HIM THROUGH
    C   B7
THE CROSS BE BORNE FOR ME, FOR YOU
  G   D
HAIL, HAIL THE WORD MADE FLESH
    C   B7   Em
THE BABE, THE SON OF MARY

  Em   D
3. SO BRING HIM INCENSE, GOLD, AND MYRRH
      C   B7
COME PEASANT, KING, TO OWN HIM
     Em   D
THE KING OF KINGS, SALVATION BRINGS
     C   B7   Em
LET LOVING HEARTS ENTHRONE HIM
  G   D
RAISE, RAISE THE SONG ON HIGH
     C   B7
THE VIRGIN SINGS HER LULLABY
  G   D
JOY, JOY, FOR CHRIST IS BORN
     C   B7   Em
THE BABE, THE SON OF MARY

WE THREE KINGS OF ORIENT ARE

John Henry Hopkins wrote the words and music for this American carol in 1857, when he was rector of Christ's Church in Williamsport, Pennsylvania. The song was part of a Christmas pageant, and his intention was that the melodic line should move like the "step of a plodding camel."

"We Three Kings" gives you yet more practice with waltz rhythm. As in "What Child Is This?" we are in a dark-sounding minor key, but at measure 17, the mood brightens—now it sounds like it's in a major key. ✦

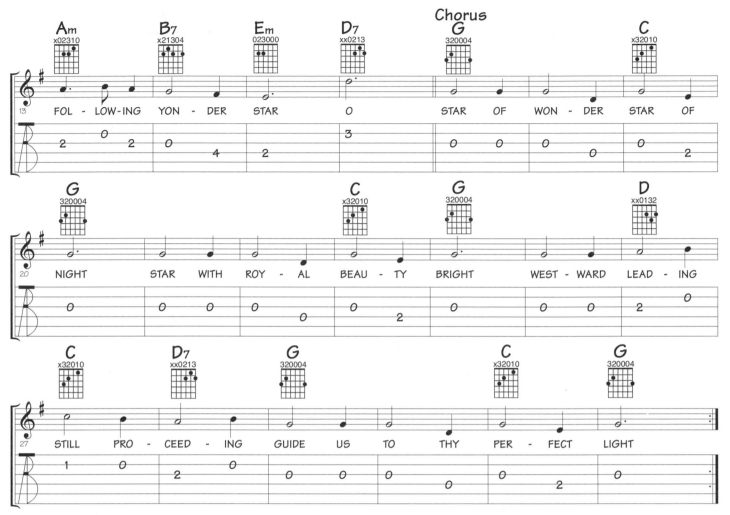

Em   B7 Em
1. WE THREE KINGS OF ORIENT ARE
        B7   Em
 BEARING GIFTS WE TRAVERSE AFAR
     D G   C
 FIELD AND FOUNTAIN, MOOR AND MOUNTAIN
Am   B7   Em
FOLLOWING YONDER STAR

   D7 G   C   G
   O STAR OF WONDER, STAR OF NIGHT
        C   G
   STAR WITH ROYAL BEAUTY BRIGHT
       D   C   D7
   WESTWARD LEADING, STILL PROCEEDING
   G   C   G
   GUIDE US TO THY PERFECT LIGHT

   Em   B7   Em
2. BORN A KING ON BETHLEHEM PLAIN
        B7   Em
 GOLD I BRING TO CROWN HIM AGAIN
      D G   C
 KING FOREVER, CEASING NEVER
Am   B7   Em
OVER US ALL TO REIGN

   CHORUS

Em   B7   Em
3. FRANKINCENSE TO OFFER HAVE I
         B7 Em
 INCENSE OWNS A DEITY NIGH
       D G   C
 PRAYER AND PRAISING, ALL MEN RAISING
Am   B7   Em
WORSHIP HIM, GOD MOST HIGH

   CHORUS

Em   B7   Em
4. MYRRH IS MINE, ITS BITTER PERFUME
         B7 Em
 BREATHES A LIFE OF GATHERING GLOOM
        D G   C
 SORROWING, SIGHING, BLEEDING, DYING
Am   B7   Em
SEALED IN THE STONE-COLD TOMB

   CHORUS

Em   B7   Em
5. GLORIOUS NOW, BEHOLD HIM ARISE
        B7 Em
 KING, AND GOD, AND SACRIFICE
       D G
 HEAVEN SINGS ALLELUIA
C Am B7 Em
ALLELUIA THE EARTH REPLIES

GOD REST YE MERRY, GENTLEMEN

In Charles Dickens' *A Christmas Carol,* Ebenezer Scrooge hears someone singing this song, picks up a ruler, and threatens to hit the singer if he does not stop immediately. Most listeners are much more appreciative of this traditional carol, said to go back as far as the 16th century.

The tempo is 4/4, which you now know as common time. Judging by the not-so-happy sound, you can probably guess that it's in a minor key. This song is by far my personal favorite. It asks for almost a military feel: to be played boldly as no one has played before.

As in "What Child Is This?" the accompaniment pattern uses a single strum per measure, this time over the span of four beats. Then in the fourth measure, the B7 chord is treated with two strums in the measure. ✦

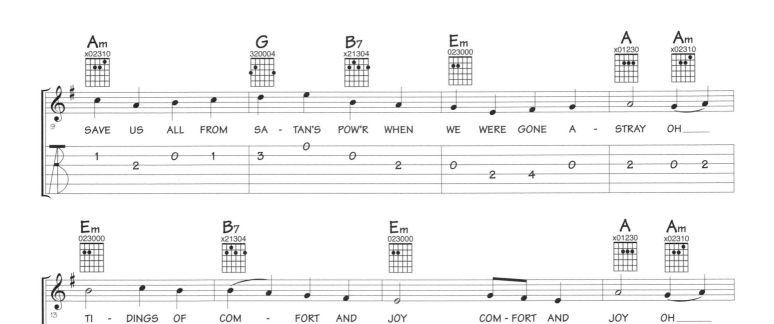

SAVE US ALL FROM SA - TAN'S POW'R WHEN WE WERE GONE A - STRAY OH____

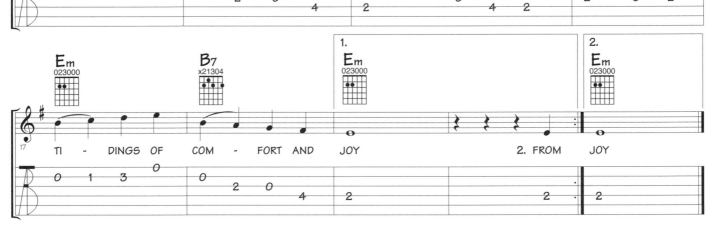

TI - DINGS OF COM - FORT AND JOY COM-FORT AND JOY OH____

1.

TI - DINGS OF COM - FORT AND JOY 2. FROM JOY

Em
1. GOD REST YE MERRY, GENTLEMEN
       C   B7
   LET NOTHING YOU DISMAY
     Em
   REMEMBER CHRIST, OUR SAVIOR,
       C   B7
   WAS BORN ON CHRISTMAS DAY
      Am   G   B7
   TO SAVE US ALL FROM SATAN'S POW'R
        Em   A
   WHEN WE WERE GONE ASTRAY
   Am Em   B7   Em   A
   O   TIDINGS OF COMFORT AND JOY, COMFORT AND JOY
   Am Em   B7   Em
   O   TIDINGS OF COMFORT AND JOY

   Em
2. FROM GOD, OUR HEAV'NLY FATHER
      C   B7
   A BLESSED ANGEL CAME
       Em
   AND UNTO CERTAIN SHEPHERDS
          C   B7
   BROUGHT TIDINGS TO THE SAME

                Am   G   B7
   HOW THAT IN BETHLEHEM WAS BORN
         Em   A
   THE SON OF GOD BY NAME
   Am Em   B7   Em   A
   O   TIDINGS OF COMFORT AND JOY, COMFORT AND JOY
   Am Em   B7   Em
   O   TIDINGS OF COMFORT AND JOY

              Em
3. IN BETHLEHEM, IN JEWRY
        C   B7
   THIS BLESSED BABE WAS BORN
        Em
   AND LAID WITHIN A MANGER
        C   B7
   UPON THIS HOLY MORN
          Am   G B7
   THE WHICH HIS MOTHER MARY
         Em   A
   DID NOTHING TAKE IN SCORN
   Am Em   B7   Em   A
   O   TIDINGS OF COMFORT AND JOY, COMFORT AND JOY
   Am Em   B7   Em
   O   TIDINGS OF COMFORT AND JOY

ANGELS WE HAVE HEARD ON HIGH

The traditional French carol "Les anges nos campagnes" was translated into English by James Chadwick in 1862.

By now you should be familiar enough with the other songs to recognize that this one is in 4/4, or common time, and that it's in a major key. "Angels" is a good review of many of the chords you've learned so far. The first part is simple enough, just G to D7 and back to G again, while the second part cycles you through a handful of chords in a progression very similar to what you learned in "Hark! The Herald Angels Sing." The accompaniment pattern is used in measures 9–16. ✦

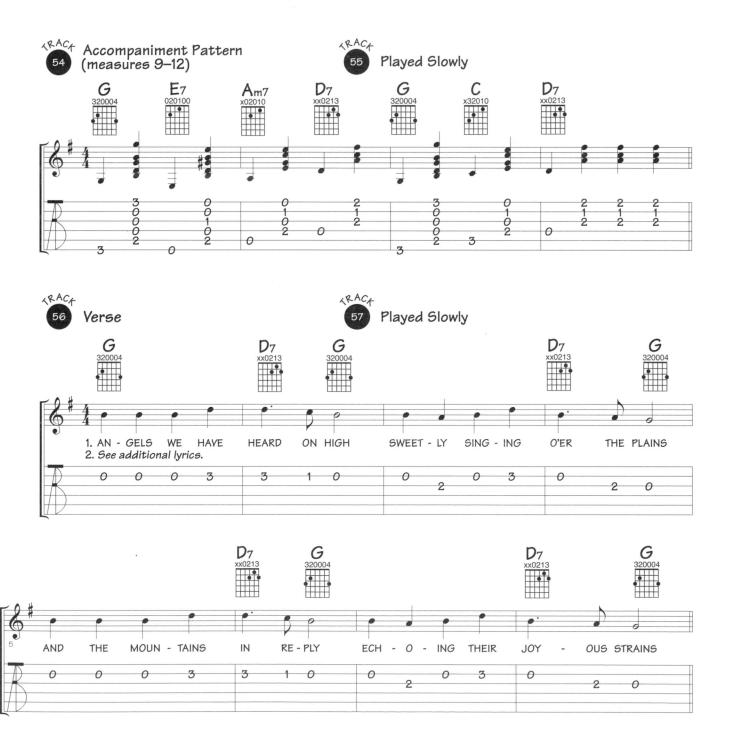

Chorus

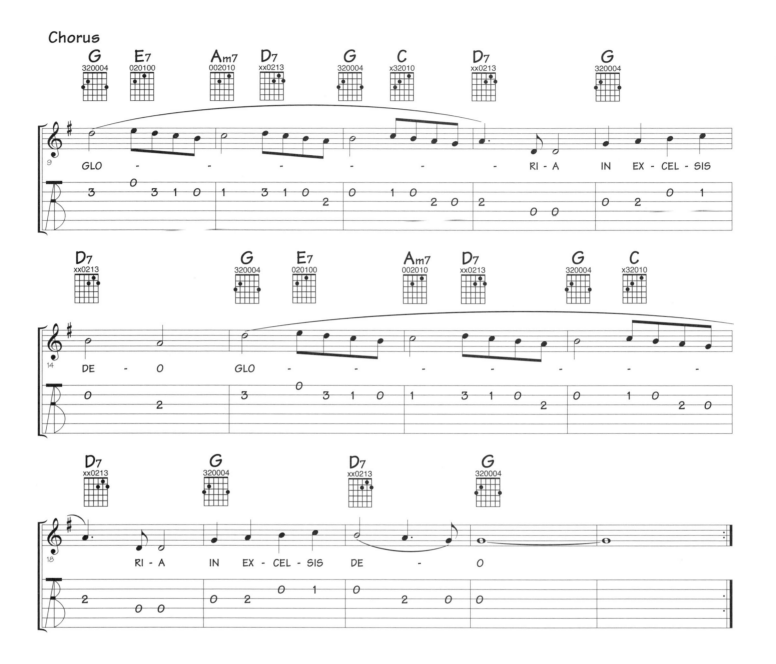

1. ANGELS WE HAVE HEARD ON HIGH
   SWEETLY SINGING O'ER THE PLAINS
   AND THE MOUNTAINS IN REPLY
   ECHOING THEIR JOYOUS STRAINS

   G E7 Am7 D7 G C D7   G   D7
   GLO - - - - - - - RIA IN EXCELSIS DEO
   G E7 Am7 D7 G C D7   G   D7 G
   GLO - - - - - - - RIA IN EXCELSIS DEO

2. SHEPHERDS, WHY THIS JUBILEE?
   WHY YOUR JOYOUS STRAINS PROLONG?
   WHAT THE GLADSOME TIDINGS BE
   WHICH INSPIRE YOUR HEAVENLY SONG?

   CHORUS

WE WISH YOU A MERRY CHRISTMAS

In old England, singers called "waits" were often hired to greet visitors, enliven weddings, and serenade holiday revelers. Many of the oldest carols, including "We Wish You a Merry Christmas," are waits' songs. Waits were often rewarded with treats like figgy pudding, which was also part of the traditional Christmas feast. It was brought into the room (sometimes on fire) as everyone sang and celebrated.

You will recognize that this song is in a major key, has a waltz feel, and is in 3/4 time. Measures 7–8 in the accompaniment pattern show how to treat measures 8–9 and the ending. It is similar to what we used in "O Christmas Tree": one short

and one long strum, followed in this case by a G strum that we hold for an entire measure.

The melody is a bit of a finger twister. Familiarize yourself with it enough to see where you're going before you get there. The fingering in measures 7 and 15 calls for your first finger to hold down the second fret of the D and G strings. One tip for learning this song: practice one line at a time. When you feel you've pretty much got one line down, practice the next, and so on, until you can put all the pieces together. ◆

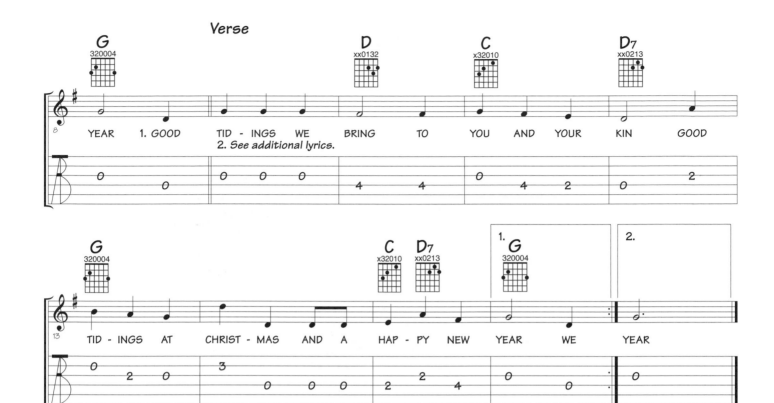

Verse

YEAR 1. GOOD TID - INGS WE BRING TO YOU AND YOUR KIN GOOD
2. See additional lyrics.

TID - INGS AT CHRIST - MAS AND A HAP - PY NEW YEAR WE YEAR

1.

2.

G   C
WE WISH YOU A MERRY CHRISTMAS
   A7   D7
WE WISH YOU A MERRY CHRISTMAS
   B7   Em
WE WISH YOU A MERRY CHRISTMAS
      C   D7   G
AND A HAPPY NEW YEAR

        G   D   C   D7
2. GOOD TIDINGS TO YOU, WHEREVER YOU ARE
            G   C   D7   G
GOOD TIDINGS FOR CHRISTMAS AND A HAPPY NEW YEAR

   CHORUS

     G   D   C   D7
1. GOOD TIDINGS WE BRING TO YOU AND YOUR KIN
       G   C   D7   G
GOOD TIDINGS AT CHRISTMAS AND A HAPPY NEW YEAR

   CHORUS

ABOUT THE AUTHOR

Peter Penhallow began playing piano and imitating Elvis Presley at the age of three, and he took up guitar at age nine. During the 13 years he was in the rock band Timmy, he cowrote and coproduced demos with Eddy Offord of Yes and Emerson, Lake, and Palmer; Andy West of the Dixie Dregs; and Vince Welnick of the Tubes. He has played in recording sessions with Mark O'Connor, Huey Lewis band members Bill Gibson and Mario Cippolina, and many others. When he is not composing, accompanying, or improvising, he enjoys producing. Penhallow has been a musical director for Children's and Community Musical Theater in Marin County, California, for 20 years and has more than 100 productions to his credit.

Keep the Holiday Spirit Going!

Holiday Songs for Fingerstyle Guitar

Bursting with tried-and-true renditions of favorites like "Silent Night" and "It Came upon a Midnight Clear," our holiday songbook is a must

By Sean McGowan

Also Available

The Alex de Grassi Fingerstyle Guitar Method

A complete course in contemporary steel-string guitar

Acoustic Guitar Solo Fingerstyle Basics

Learn the fundamentals of solo fingerstyle guitar

Roots and Blues Fingerstyle Guitar

Blues fingerpicking and slide techniques you can use

Fingerstyle Blues

15 essential blues arrangements in a variety of styles

Fingerstyle Jazz Guitar Essentials

Learn the art of fingerstyle jazz guitar with Sean McGowan

Sottish Songs For Guitar

A collection of 15 Scottish fingerstyle classics

Irish Songs For Guitar

Danny Carnahan's 15 favorite Irish songs arranged for acoustic guitar

Spanish Repertoire For Classical Guitar

Learn Spanish classical pieces from Francisco Tarrega, Julian Arcas, and more

Children's Songs For Beginning Guitar

Peter Penhallow teaches 15 beloved children's tunes

Early Jazz and Swing Songs For Guitar

15 must-know jazz and swing standards for guitar

---

store.AcousticGuitar.com

More Tools to Get You Started

Let the bestselling *Acoustic Guitar Method* by David Hamburger be your guide to the joys of playing the guitar.

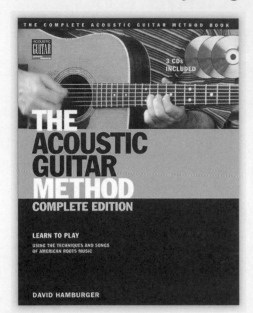

The COMPLETE Acoustic Guitar Method

The *Acoustic Guitar Method* is the only beginning guitar method based on traditional American music that teaches you authentic techniques and songs. From the folk and blues music of yesterday have come the rock, country, and jazz of today. Understand, play, and enjoy these essential traditions and styles on the instrument that truly represents American music, the acoustic guitar. This comprehensive approach is the one tool you need to get started. **$24.95**, 136 pp., 9" x 12", HL00695667

Acoustic Guitar Method, Book One

LESSONS First Chords, First Song | New Chord, New Strum | Tab Basics and Your First Melody | Reading Notes | The G Chord | The C Chord | More Single Notes | Country Backup Basics | Seventh Chords | Waltz Time | Half Notes and Rests | Minor Chords | A Minor-Key Melody | The B7 Chord.
SONGS Columbus Stockade Blues | Careless Love | Darling Corey | East Virginia Blues | In the Pines | Banks of the Ohio | Scarborough Fair | Shady Grove | Man of Constant Sorrow | and more!
$9.95, 48 pp., 9" x 12", HL00695648

Acoustic Guitar Method, Book Two

LESSONS The Alternating Bass | Blues in E | Major Scales and Melodies | Starting to Fingerpick | More Picking Patterns | The G-Major Scale | Bass Runs | More Bass Runs | Blues Basics | Alternating-Bass Fingerpicking | Fingerpicking in 3/4.
SONGS Columbus Stockade Blues | Stagolee | The Girl I Left Behind Me | Shady Grove | Shenandoah | Will the Circle Be Unbroken? | Sail Away Ladies | I Am a Pilgrim | Bury Me Beneath the Willow | Alberta | Sugar Babe | House of the Rising Sun.
$9.95, 48 pp., 9" x 12", HL00695649

Acoustic Guitar Method, Book Three

LESSONS The Swing Feel | Tackling the F Chord | More Chord Moves | Introducing Travis Picking | Travis Picking, Continued | Hammer-ons, Slides, and Pull-offs | Alternate Bass Notes | The Pinch | All Together Now.
SONGS Frankie and Johnny | Delia | Gambler's Blues | Banks of the Ohio | Crawdad | New River Train | Sail Away Ladies | Little Sadie | Omie Wise | That'll Never Happen No More.
$9.95, 48 pp., 9" x 12", HL00695666

Dive Deeper into Chords, Slide, and Jazz

Learn authentic techniques and expand your understanding of musical essentials

The Acoustic Guitar Method Chord Book

David Hamburger's supplementary chord book for the *Acoustic Guitar Method* is a must-have resource for building your chord vocabulary! Start with a user-friendly explanation of what chords are and how they are named, then learn chords by key in all 12 keys, with both open-position and closed-position voicings for each common chord type.
$5.95, 48 pp., 9" x 12", HL00695722

Acoustic Guitar Slide Basics

Bitten by the blues bug? Want to explore the haunting sounds of acoustic slide guitar or brush up on your bottleneck basics? This easy-to-follow, step-by-step book and CD will help you master one of the great styles of American roots music. LESSONS | Single-String Melodies | Working in the Thumb | Moving Around the Neck | Spicing Up Your Melodies | Travis Picking | and more!
$16.95, 72 pp., 9" x 12", HL00695610

Early Jazz and Swing Songs for Guitar

Add early jazz and swing standards to your repertoire! Learn full guitar parts, read detailed notes on the song origins, and hear a two-guitar recording of each tune. SONGS After You've Gone | Avalon | Baby, Won't You Please Come Home | Ballin' the Jack | Hindustan | Limehouse Blues | Rose Room | Saint James Infirmary | St. Louis Blues | Whispering | and more! **$9.95**, 40 pp., 9" x 12", HL00695867

Buy online at store.AcousticGuitar.com